PLANTS SEEDS and FLOWERS

Troll Associates

PLANTS SEEDS and FLOWERS

by Louis Sabin

Illustrated by Holly Moylan

Troll Associates

Library of Congress Cataloging in Publication Data

Sabin, Louis.
    Plants, seeds, and flowers.

    Summary: Describes briefly the evolution of plants,
the different types of seeds they produce, and how
seeds travel, take root, and reproduce.
    1. Plants—Juvenile literature.   2. Seeds—Juvenile
literature.   3. Flowers—Juvenile literature.   [1. Plants.
2. Seeds.   3. Flowers]   I. Moylan, Holly, ill.   II. Title.
QK49.S25   1984   582   84-2720
ISBN 0-8167-0226-8 (lib. bdg.)
ISBN 0-8167-0227-6 (pbk.)

A vast field of wheat ripples like a golden sea. Shiny red apples hang heavy on the trees in the orchard, while a forest of blue-green spruce trees covers a nearby mountainside. A bright yellow rose sends a sweet scent into the summer air, while a thick mat of green algae drifts on the surface of a pond. Deep in the jungle, a thick vine winds around the trunk of a rubber tree. And far out in the desert, a cactus plant stands like a lonely sentry.

Every one of these growing things looks different from the others. But they are all related to each other. They are all members of the plant family. And it is a huge family, indeed, with more than 350,000 species in it. These species range from the tiny, one-celled algae to the huge redwood tree that stands as tall as a thirty-six-story building.

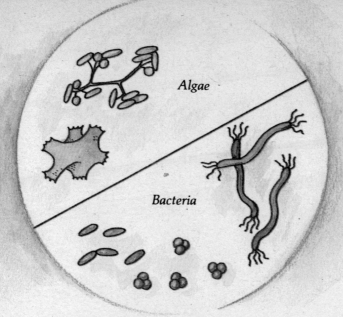

Algae

Bacteria

Plants have been on Earth for a much longer time than insects or birds or any other animals. The first plants may have appeared two billion years ago. They were only simple bacteria and algae that lived in the waters covering much of the world. But they were the ancestors of all the plants that grow on Earth today.

Many millions of years passed. New forms of plants that could live on land appeared. They were still simple compared to the flowering shrubs and the trees we know today. But those first land plants were very much like the ferns and mosses that grow in damp, shady places in modern forests.

Those first land plants had no seeds and no true roots. Like the mushrooms, toadstools, and other forms of fungus plants that developed at about the same time, the ferns and mosses contained *spores*. Spores are microscopic cells that are a little like seeds. But they do not have a protective coating, as seeds do. Because spores are unprotected, they cannot stay alive for long. They must fall in a place with perfect conditions in order to become a plant.

If a spore lands in a place that is dry, it will die. A seed, because it is protected, can last much longer. And when the right conditions for growth occur, it begins to take root.

The first seed plants appeared about 300 million years ago. They were conifers—plants with cones containing a number of seeds. The early conifers were very much like today's pine, fir, and spruce trees.

The seeds in a conifer form after the egg cells inside the cone are fertilized. They are fertilized by wind-blown pollen that comes from other trees of the same kind. Fir pollen fertilizes only fir eggs. Spruce pollen can only fertilize spruce eggs. And so on.

Conifers must produce many more pollen cells than egg cells. That is because the egg cells stay safe inside the cone, while the pollen cells are blown in all directions by the wind. A pond in a pine or spruce forest may look as if it had been painted yellow at pollination time. The yellow coating on the water is really countless billions of pollen grains from the trees.

When pollen cells are blown by the wind into a cone, they fertilize the egg cells. The egg cells then grow into seeds. These seeds are protected by the hard cone until they are ripe. Then the cone opens and the seeds fall to the ground. In time, a few seeds may take root and grow into new trees.

15

Flowering plants have existed for only half as long as conifers. One of the first flowering plants was the magnolia. The magnolia was different from conifers because both pollen cells and egg cells grew next to each other in the same flower. For this reason, the magnolia did not need the undependable wind to carry its seeds. All it needed for fertilization was an insect to carry the pollen a very short distance to the egg cells.

The relationship of insects to flowering plants has been so successful that it hasn't changed in 150 million years. To survive, a flowering plant—such as the magnolia tree or a rose—must attract insects by showing bright-colored flowers or giving off pleasing smells.

The insects want the nectar that is in the flower, so they search for the sights and smells that lead them to the nectar.

As the insect feeds on the nectar, some grains of pollen stick to its body. Sometimes this pollen rubs off on the flower's egg cells as the insect moves around. Or, when the insect flies to another flower, it passes on the pollen it has just picked up. In this way, while flowers feed insects, insects pollinate flowering plants.

Once the pollen has done its job of fertilizing the plant's egg cells, a change takes place. The plant no longer needs the brightly colored flower. So the petals drop off. This is called "going to seed." Now the food that the plant used to produce the flower can be used to feed the fertilized egg cells. And the seeds for another generation of flowers can develop and ripen.

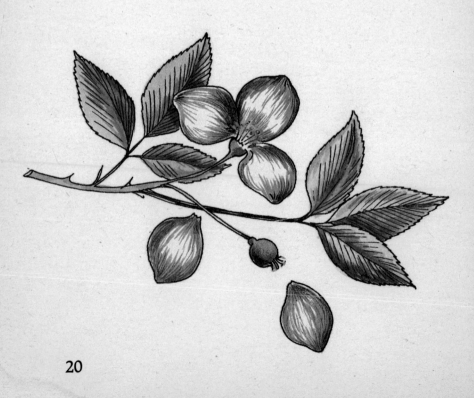

The next step in the plant's life cycle is to spread its seeds. This happens in different ways, depending on the species of the plant.

When a dandelion goes to seed, its yellow flower is replaced by a fluffy ball of tiny seeds. Each seed is attached to a feathery, white tuft that is like an umbrella turned inside out. The wind catches these light tufts and carries them away, sometimes miles away.

The seeds of the maple tree are contained in pods that are wing-shaped. They drift and spin like propellers in the autumn wind. The oak seed, in its tough-shelled acorn, is spread by small animals such as squirrels.

Just as insects do not know they are carrying pollen from flower to flower, squirrels do not know they are helping new plants to grow. They bury acorns for their own use. But they bury far more acorns than they will ever eat. Most of the acorns remain buried. Some of them will take root, become oak trees, and grow acorns that will feed other squirrels.

The seeds of many plants are found inside soft, fleshy growths called fruits. In some cases, we eat the fruit but not the seed. This is true when we eat apples, pears, cherries, peaches, and melons, and throw away the seeds. But the seeds of strawberries, blueberries, tomatoes, and bananas are so small and soft that we eat them with the fruit.

Stages of a seed's germination

When a plant seed reaches the ground, it may sprout right away, or months may pass before it starts to sprout. Most seeds that fall from a plant in the summer or autumn do not sprout, or germinate, until the next spring. Then, when the weather is warm enough and the ground is moist and soft, the seed coat splits open and germination begins.

When a plant germinates, roots are sent down into the soil. There, they take in water and minerals. At the same time, the plant is using the food stored in its seed to grow a stem and its first pale leaves. It needs the stored food to stay alive until it is rooted and has leaves.

As plants grow, they make their own food in their leaves. It is done through a process called *photosynthesis*. In photosynthesis, which means "putting together with light," the leaves use sunlight to change water and a gas called carbon dioxide into food. Then the food is spread throughout the plant.

The action of photosynthesis does not take place in the whole plant. It takes place only in the leaves. That is because the leaves have a substance called *chlorophyll* that makes photosynthesis possible. It is also chlorophyll that gives a plant its green color.

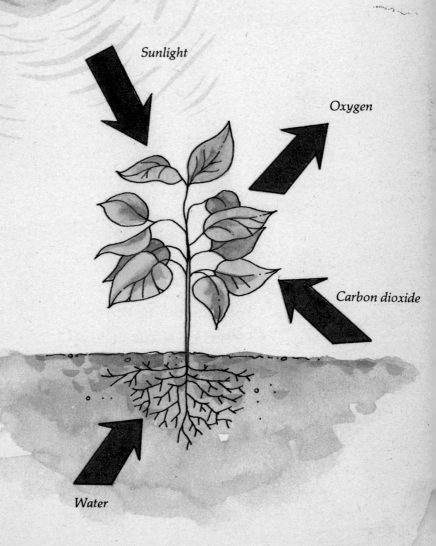

Photosynthesis

Sunlight

Oxygen

Carbon dioxide

Water

The food made in plants is a kind of sugar. In fact, most of the sugar we use comes from a plant called sugar cane. And it is because of sugar that the syrup tapped from maple trees is sweet. Sugar is also what gives sweetness to such plants as carrots, grapes, corn, and watermelon.

A plant uses its food to grow and thrive. When it has reached maturity, it flowers. After the flowering stage, the plant goes to seed. The plant's seeds drop to the ground and, in time, may germinate. And so, as it has been for millions of years, the life cycle of a plant goes on.